The Final Twist

A play

Ken Whitmore
and Alfred Bradley

Samuel French — London
New York - Toronto - Hollywood

NCR·PP

Please see page iv for further copyright information

THE FINAL TWIST

First produced on BBC Radio Four on 30th March, 1996
with the following cast:

Sir Merlin Foster	Donald Sinden
Charlie Nicholson	Michael Troughton
Eden Dundee	Amanda Waring
Morten Rifles	John Hartley

Produced and directed by Eynd Williams

CHARACTERS

Sir Merlin Foster, an actor in his sixties
Charlie Nicholson, a writer in his thirties
Eden Dundee, Merlin's wife, aged twenty-three
Morten Rifles, age and profession confidential*

* Morten Rifles may be played by Merlin Foster in disguise or another actor. If one actor is playing both it is important to give a name in the theatre programme for 'the actor' playing Morten Rifles (an anagram for Merlin Foster) or the cat will be let out of the bag.

Other plays by Ken Whitmore published by
Samuel French Ltd

La Bolshie Vita
Jump For Your Life
Pen-Friends
The Turn of the Screw (*adapt. from James*)

Other plays by Alfred Bradley published by
Samuel French Ltd

The Adventures of a Bear Called Paddington
(*adapt. from Bond*)
The Nightingale and the Emperor
The Scatterbrained Scarecrow of Oz
The Wizard of Oz (*adapt. from Baum*)

SYNOPSIS OF SCENES

The action takes place in the living-room of Merlin Foster's country cottage, fifty miles from London, over the course of a month

ACT I
SCENE 1   Mid morning
SCENE 2   3 a.m. A week later

ACT II
SCENE 1   Dusk. A week later
SCENE 2   Late evening the following Saturday

Time — the present

For Hope Whitmore
and
In memory of Alfred

ACT I

SCENE 1

Before the CURTAIN *rises there is a sparkling performance of the opening of Mozart's 40th Symphony*

The living-room of Merlin Foster's very tasteful cottage fifty miles from London. It is mid morning

There is a television, sofa, drinks cabinet, and a desk with a drawer containing a revolver and a small black cassette player. On the desk is a box of cigars, telephone, pen, pencil and paper. Good modern paintings are on the walls and a shelf of books that use two of Merlin's Oscars as bookends. The front door is at rear stage C *and a door to the kitchen at* R. *An open staircase leads to the upstairs*

As the CURTAIN *rises the music is replaced by the chime of an electric doorbell that plays the first twenty notes of the same symphony*

In response to the chimes Merlin Foster comes thumping downstairs in his dressing-gown

Merlin (*opening the front door and roaring jovially*) Ah, Charlie? Charlie Nicholson? Good! Good to see you! Now come on in!

Merlin brings Charlie into the living-room

Awfully kind of you to come traipsing out all this way.

Charlie lives on the desperate fringe of the literary world and has a haircut, clothes and temperament to match. The clothes are a leather jacket, jeans and trainers, all from Oxfam. He looks about in awe at the exquisite interior. Merlin is coolly amused and observant. He has the tremendous style and gravitas of an old matinee idol who has matured into a national monument

Charlie Thank you, Sir Merlin, it's a great — um — it's a very great privilege to — um ——

Merlin To meet me? Yes, I know. And it's an honour to have you here, my dear boy.

Charlie Gosh. Well. Here I am. Face to face with Merlin Foster. Oh, do I call you sir or what?

Merlin Just call me Merlin.

Charlie (*with a gesture to the door*) And so that's the doorbell.

Merlin I'm sorry?

Charlie That's the doorbell.

Merlin What about it?

Charlie Mozart's 40th. (*Humming it*) Tiddy-bum tiddy-bum tiddy-bum-bum.

Merlin Yes, that's right.

Charlie I've heard that before.

Merlin You've heard Mozart's 40th?

Charlie I've heard that doorbell.

Merlin You've heard my doorbell? What, before today? I don't quite follow.

Charlie Yes — when you rang me up — remember?

Merlin Ah!

Charlie In the middle of our conversation I suddenly heard Mozart's 40th in a very — you know — esoteric arrangement and then you said, "Excuse me, Charlie, someone's at the door."

Merlin Did I really?

Charlie And I said to myself, "Good heavens, that must be his doorbell." (*Humming it*) Tiddy-bum tiddy-bum tiddy-bum-bum.

Merlin Yes. Listen, why do you keep going on about my bloody doorbell?

Charlie I'm nervous. I used to see you up there on the silver screen when I was a boy. You're a legend. I'm just — nervous.

Merlin Nothing to be nervous about.

Charlie God, what a wonderful cottage. You live here all the time?

Merlin Eh? Oh, no, just at weekends. We've a little pad in London. Sit down, Charlie, relax. Something to drink? Tea, coffee, something stronger?

Charlie Eh? Oh no, I'm fine, fine.

Merlin Did you follow all my instructions?

Charlie Yes. Yes, I did.

Merlin Told nobody you were coming here?

Charlie Not a soul, no, nobody.

Merlin Not your agent?

Charlie Nobody at all.

Merlin Splendid. Good man.

Charlie No. (*Pause*) Look — um — I don't quite follow what we're supposed to be up to.

Merlin Up to? Ah, up to.

Charlie gapes at him open-mouthed

Well —— (*He stops in exasperation*) Charlie, I wish you wouldn't gape at me like that.

Charlie Sorry. I still can't get used to it. Me — here — with Sir Merlin Foster. Big in films, big on the stage. Married five times to five of the most wonderful — the classiest — the sexiest — oh, I do beg your pardon.

Merlin Six wives actually. Can you name them all, I wonder?

Charlie Name them? Well, let me see — there was that beautiful Swedish blonde film star ——

Merlin Danish.

Charlie Danish, yes. Petra Borg, that's right. Then — let me see — the baked beans billionairess. Right? Then Rosalind Underhill. Myra Stringer, of course. God, imagine being married to Rosalind Underhill. Now let me see — did you ever marry Elizabeth Taylor?

Merlin Elizabeth Taylor? I can't recall.

Charlie Can't recall? Oh, that's a good one! Married to Elizabeth Taylor and can't recall!

Merlin I have a rather poor memory. And do you remember any more of my wives?

Charlie Well if you can't how do you expect me … wait a minute. Then you married — oh, her name's on the tip of my tongue. Dorothea Southgate, the Catholic novelist. And she's your wife now. I saw a picture of the pair of you — oh — quite recently. Dorothea Southgate, the female Graham Greene.

Merlin Oh no. You're wrong there. Dorothea Southgate divorced me a couple of years ago.

Charlie She divorced you?

Merlin Yes.

Charlie That's strange.

Merlin What's strange about it?

Charlie Well, that picture, in the paper. And then she's a Catholic.

Merlin Right.

Charlie I thought they couldn't divorce.

Merlin (*with great bitterness*) She got a papal dispensation.

Charlie Ah. Oh, I see. (*Pause*) There's something that's always puzzled me.

Merlin About me?

Charlie Yes, I could never quite work out whether you were British or American. You have that sort of international ——

Merlin (*with sad gravity and utter conviction*) Where do I come from? I have trouble remembering. It was all so long ago and I've been so many people in my time. My father was a cannibal king up the Amazon. He ate an entire British Council touring company of *Dear Octopus* — with the exception of the property mistress, who fascinated him with her thunder machine and lightning flashes and coloured smokes. In due course she gave birth to me

and when I was seven years old we managed to escape at the height of the
monsoon season. I rather miss the old boy. No, that's not true. I miss him
dreadfully. He was the only civilized man I ever encountered.

Charlie Er, yes — so what did you want with me, Sir Merlin?

Merlin I want you to write me a play.

Charlie Me? You want *me* to write a play for *you*? But I'm — nobody. I'm
so obscure. Anyway, I couldn't write a play for you.

Merlin Why not?

Charlie I've got a block — a creative block.

Merlin Oh?

Charlie I stopped writing in nineteen-ninety-six. I just fizzled out. It was my
annus horribilis — you know? — like the Queen.

Merlin What happened?

Charlie Well, my wife divorced me, then my novel was rejected and then
to cap it all my first play closed after a week. Oh, and apart from that I lost
nine thousand pounds gambling.

Merlin Lost nine thousand pounds?

Charlie Yes.

Merlin You managed to repay it?

Charlie No, that's the trouble. There's a bookie in Manchester — he's hired
a thug to come and get it off me. What they call an enforcer.

Merlin Good heavens.

Charlie I have to keep changing my address.

Merlin Good Lord. What can he do — this thug?

Charlie Depends on the bookie — whether he wants me pine-boxed or just
badly hurt.

Merlin Good God. Pine-boxed? I'd no idea you were a fugitive. Can't you
write something and pay the bugger off?

Charlie I've tried. But I'm like a rabbit — paralysed in the headlights. Can't
write any more. There's a great big hollow where my brain used to be. No
ideas any more. No nothing.

Merlin *I* have an idea.

Charlie You have an idea?

Merlin Yes. I have an idea.

Charlie For a play?

Merlin For a play, yes, a play.

Charlie Ah — so you want me to write it?

Merlin Yes, I do.

Charlie It's still no good. I've been sort of — castrated — for writing. I've
got a block as big as Beachy Head.

Merlin Listen, Charlie, act as if you had faith and it will be given to you.

Charlie Oh, if only.

Merlin These problems can be overcome. I know. I was in therapy myself for fifteen years. I always recall the moment I said goodbye to my shrink. I remember our parting words. I said to him, "Will I always be nuts, Tony?" And he replied, "Merlin, I hope so."

Charlie (*regarding him suspiciously*) Yes.

Merlin Rum world. Must be a God, you know. How else explain fellows like me and Michelangelo? On the day God made me everything must have been absolutely on song in the heavenly workshops. He turns out great batches of ordinary types, but just now and then the machines are at perfect pitch and along comes a Mozart or a Merlin Foster. When I come face to face with the great playwright in the sky I shall say, "My Dear Fellow, thank You for the starring role, there were so many bit parts. What a jolly interesting piece, but what was it all about? Was there a message?" I'm sorry. Must be bloody horrible to be you. Hard luck, old son.

Charlie Thanks. Very much. (*Pause*) So what is this idea of yours? Not that I can promise anything — what with my head like this.

Merlin I want you to work out a foolproof plan for me to murder my wife.

Charlie Murder your wife? (*Pause*) You mean a play? A murder play?

Merlin Yes.

Charlie A thriller? For you? Merlin Foster?

Merlin Just so. A thriller.

Charlie For you to play in?

Merlin Yes.

Charlie But — but look here — but you're a man of the classics. Good heavens, your Hamlet, your Cyrano, your Willie Loman, we were brought up on you.

Merlin Have you ever heard of alimony? Of the tax man?

Charlie Alimony?

Merlin Six marriages, Charlie. Those women have pauperized me. But still I dream, Charlie. As you were so kind to say, I'm about to hit my perihelion. My very perihelion. And I want to go out in style, Charlie, I want to play Lear, Prospero, Falstaff and the Jew of Malta in one coruscating, scintillating season. It'll be the cherry on top of my knickerbocker glory. And then — puff — the comet called Merlin Foster can fall from the heavens. But that takes money. So to pay for it I need one tacky thriller.

Charlie And I supply the tacky thriller.

Merlin Come slumming, Charlie. I'll make it worth your while. Twenty thousand up front.

Charlie Pounds?

Merlin Twenty thousand. Tax free. And twenty thousand more on acceptance of the final script.

Charlie For a plot — hang on — for a plot — to murder your wife?

Merlin Yes.

Charlie We are talking about a play?

Merlin What else? Oh, I see! No, no, I adore my wife. You'll soon find out. You'll be meeting her very shortly. She's just out for a gallop at present.

Charlie Gallop?

Merlin Yes, on a horse.

Charlie Oh, a horse, yes. (*Pause*) Forty thousand pounds? Do you mind if I call my agent?

Merlin Yes, I do mind.

Charlie I can't speak to my agent?

Merlin I've spoken to him.

Charlie Oh? What did he say?

Merlin Said you were no good.

Charlie No good? Henry Savage said I was no good?

Merlin Said you were a born loser and you'd never trouble the scoreboard.

Charlie Henry?

Merlin First of all, when I said I wanted you to write me a thriller, Savage offered me another writer.

Charlie Another writer?

Merlin Who happens to be his son-in-law. Then when I said it had to be Charlie Nicholson or nobody he offered me a deal.

Charlie What kind of deal?

Merlin The author of a stage play normally takes seven per cent of the box office. Savage said I could have you for five.

Charlie Five per cent? What are you talking about?

Merlin Plus one per cent for Savage under the counter. And one per cent for me. In other words he planned to rob you of two per cent. And with the production I have in mind that would mean you'd be losing about forty thousand pounds a year.

Charlie Forty thousand a year?

Merlin Just scribble this little piece of fluff and I promise you your take will be a hundred and fifty thousand, at least.

Charlie And you put this to Henry? And he said I'd never trouble the scoreboard? I didn't know he was a cricket fan. So what did you do?

Merlin I accepted the son-in-law.

Charlie Accepted the ——

Merlin I commissioned a play from the son-in-law. It cost me five thousand pounds. It will be a travesty. We signed the contract yesterday.

Charlie Why did you do that — five thousand pounds for a travesty?

Merlin To throw Savage off the scent.

Charlie Scent? What scent?

Merlin The scent of the great fortune we're about to make. It's obvious Savage is not a man to be trusted. I don't want him to get wind of my idea.

Charlie The idea that you murder your wife? Look — you're sure this is just a play?

Merlin Dearest child, I'm Merlin Zacharias Foster, the greatest living actor. I've achieved all a man *can* aspire to and I'm on course for a slab in Westminster Ab. Do you think I'd risk all that for the sake of a tawdry murder?

Charlie Then why all this — this ——

Merlin Secrecy? Because we're talking about a multi-million pound business. It's called the theatre and it feeds off ideas. Ideas are golden. That's why they have to be guarded like atomic secrets. I have one, Charlie. I have an idea and I don't want it stolen by the likes of Henry Savage. A good new thriller will run for ever, Charlie. One set, small cast, low costs, astronomical profits. I produce, cast and star in it myself. They'll come in droves to see me. They always have. It will take a couple of years out of my life and make me comfortable for ever. It will make *you* comfortable for ever. Just think of it, Charlie — irrevocable wealth.

Charlie Irrevocable wealth? (*Pause*) Tell me more. What is this idea?

Merlin The idea is this. A terribly celebrated old actor manager like me hires a starving young writer like you to invent a plot to murder his wife. Now tell me — what is the most vital ingredient of a successful play?

Charlie Well — a story.

Merlin Go on.

Charlie A good strong story.

Merlin Go on.

Charlie With the ring of truth. With authenticity.

Merlin We're getting there. Anything else?

Charlie With convincing characters. Real people.

Merlin Real people! He's got it. Real places. Real situations. Write me a murder, Charlie. One that could work in real life because it's based on real people, on my old lady and me. Study me. Study my wife. Study our habits. Study this cottage and our little house in Knightsbridge. Winkle out where in all this web of relationships the perfect crime could be committed. I want a complete blueprint with calculations accurate to one billionth of one degree and then we'll put it on the test bench.

Charlie Test bench? How do you mean?

Merlin I mean I'll carry out your plan to the letter. I'll get hold of the cut throat razor or the meat cleaver or whichever blunt instrument you choose, Or look here — hold on to your hat — I'll show you something. (*He takes a revolver from a drawer*) Perhaps this would come in handy.

Charlie Is that real?

Merlin Yes, it's a point thirty-two calibre revolver, six bullets in the chamber.

Charlie Live ones?

Merlin Of course live ones. This is a lonely spot. I don't intend having my career cut short by the first young dopehead who comes out here wanting money to buy wacky baccy.

Charlie Um — would you mind? — I should put it away now.

Merlin If it alarms you.(*He puts the gun back in the drawer*) But bear it in mind.

Charlie Yes — um — sorry to bring this up, but I'll need an advance. I do have to eat.

Merlin Of course you do. A writer should eat like a king. (*He gets his chequebook from the desk*) Would five thousand be enough to be going on with?

Charlie Well — should keep me in pencils and paper.

Merlin There you are. Don't put it on a horse. Actually I don't care what you do with it. It's really nothing to do with me. As long as you don't spend it all at the Barracuda Club.

Charlie Barracuda Club?

Merlin The local gambling palace, just by the station.

Charlie What, a casino?

Merlin Never you mind. Forget I ever mentioned it. And put that cheque away before my wife comes in.

Charlie Why? Doesn't she know about this?

Merlin Good God, no. That would spoil everything. No, no, dear boy, my wife must be the complete innocent — wickedly plotted against and totally in the dark, so that we can witness her horrified reactions as the truth slowly — ah! — listen — that's her at the door now, I do believe. Now remember, mum's the word.

The front door opens and Eden hurries in, deeply upset. She's a lovely girl wearing riding clothes and carrying a riding crop and hard hat

Eden Oh, Merlin, something terrible's happened.

She rushes up to him and weeps on his shoulder

Merlin What is it? What is it?

Eden It's poor old Jimmy Thimble. He's gone and broken his knees. It will mark him for life.

Merlin Oh, dear dear dear.

Eden I had to wait for the vet and he took absolutely ages and then — (*spotting Charlie*) — oh — sorry — how do you do?

Charlie Oh — good, good.

Merlin Eden Dundee, aspiring actress. Funny name, isn't it, but she comes from there. Dundee, I mean, not Eden. Oh, I don't know, though. (*Pinching her cheek*) Little temptress.

Eden Give over, Merlin. Jimmy's hurt himself quite badly. He trod on a stone on Bonfire Hill. It was hidden under all that horrible bracken. I could tell straight away something was wrong.

Merlin Darling, can't this wait for a moment? We have a guest.

Eden Sorry, only I'm so upset. I'm going to have to stay down here for a few days and look after him, Merlin. The girls at the stable are very kind and well-intentioned but they can't give him the love and attention. I'm sorry, Mr erm ——

Merlin Charlie Nicholson.

Eden Sorry, Mr Nicholson, you must think I'm terribly ——

Charlie No no, no, I understand.

Eden Yes — well — I'll go up and get out of these jodhpurs. Excuse me. (*Starting to go, then coming back*) Did you say Charlie Nicholson? You aren't by any chance *the* Charlie Nicholson?

Charlie (*decidedly*) No.

Eden No?

Charlie I don't think so.

Eden Did you write *The Black Telephone Box*?

Charlie (*tickled pink*) Yes.

Eden *The Mysterious Refrigerator?*

Charlie Yes.

Eden They're fabulous, utterly fabulous.

Charlie Oh, get away. They're a complete waste of trees.

Eden But they're wonderful. A bit on the gruesome side, but what the hell, what's a bit of gore these days, no?

Merlin (*suddenly suspicious*) Now wait a moment. Just wait a moment.

Eden Yes?

Merlin Where did *you* come across Charlie's books?

Eden Charlie's books? In your study — at Kinnerton Street. Why ——

Merlin Kinnerton — ? Oh. Oh, I see.

Eden Are you going to commission a play from him? A lovely juicy murder story with a poor lovely lady cut in pieces and posted to all points of the compass? Oh, do, Merlin, I think you'd make a divine murderer.

Merlin (*scandalized*) A murderer? Me?

Eden Oh go on. You'd be a wonderful murderer.

Merlin My dear, I'm an artist, a man of the classics. Putting Merlin Foster in a murder mystery would be like trying to cram a bird of paradise into a canary cage. Besides, Charlie's given up murder. He's into the theatre of significance.

Eden Oh, no, how terrible. I think you should stick to murder, Charlie, because after all so many people have done that other kind of thing, haven't they? No? Righto, I'll pop up and change. You think about what I said, the pair of you.

She goes off upstairs

Merlin Well? You like?

Charlie Not half. She's very nice. Um — as a matter of interest, how old …
Merlin She's just twenty-three. I got her fresh out of drama school. Still wet
from her first Shakespeare. Does she give you any ideas?
Charlie Ideas? No!
Merlin For the play.
Charlie Oh. What, already? I'm not a slot machine. Plays don't pop out like
chewing gum, you know.
Merlin That's a good one! "Plays don't pop out like chewing gum." Make
a note of that. We want plenty of that. Concrete images. And the murder
must arise quite naturally out of Eden's daily routine, so study her closely.
You could stay here for the next week or two. That fall in with your plans?
Charlie Very nicely, thank you.
Merlin Eden's stopping down here to nurse the horse. Good, good. Couldn't
have worked out better. You could get to know her intimately.
Charlie Yes, I could.
Merlin Look, I've got to be back in town in an hour to see Dickie
Attenborough. Would you care for a lift?
Charlie Back to town?
Merlin Yes, to collect your things.
Charlie Yes, please.
Merlin I'll tell you what — I could show you round our house in Kinnerton
Street at the same time. You could drown her in the jacuzzi. (*He chuckles
at his own joke*) Listen, you could meet our neighbours — the old Duchess
of Lonsdale and the Police Commissioner.
Charlie Police Commissioner?
Merlin We live next door to the Commissioner of Police at Scotland Yard,
Sir Norman Macnamara. He's a great friend of ours. You could put him
into the plot. Well think about it. Now let me consult my diary and see the
best time for you to move in here. (*He consults a diary on the desk*) I fly
to Venice next Wednesday for the Bertolucci film. Away for ten days. You
should have a good chunk of the script ready by the time I get home.
Charlie Me? Some hopes.
Merlin Well I've given you plenty to chew on. Oh, talking of ideas, you
haven't seen the well at the bottom of the garden.
Charlie Well?
Merlin Old artesian well. Tailor made for dead bodies. Go and take a look
at it. And while you're out there you'd better make notes of this conversation.
Charlie Notes? What for?
Merlin What for? Why, to use in the play. Make notes of all our conversations.
Make notes of everything.
Charlie I don't normally make notes for a play.
Merlin This is not a normal play. So make notes. Real people, real places,
real dialogue. Now off you go.

Charlie Which way?
Merlin Through the kitchen door, there, see, down the path, through the kissing gate. Can't miss it. Well off you go, dear boy! What am I paying you for?

Charlie goes off through the kitchen door, humming Mozart's 40th

Merlin takes a cigar from the box on the desk and lights it

Eden comes downstairs in a nice frock

Eden Where's Charlie?
Merlin In Brazil where the nuts come from.
Eden (*too young for this ancient joke*) Brazil?
Merlin He's in the garden. I say, is that a new frock?
Eden Yes.
Merlin How much?
Eden It's Zandra Rhodes.
Merlin I didn't ask whose it was. I asked the price.
Eden Since when did you bother about the cost of a thousand pound frock?
Merlin A thousand pounds?
Eden Merlin, I've seen you tip a waiter fifty for a good table, so don't lecture me. What's the matter, darling? Has something gone wrong?
Merlin We've just folded on Broadway.
Eden Oh no.
Merlin I've told Herman to put up the closing notices.
Eden Oh, no, Merlin, I'm so sorry.
Merlin So is my accountant. It appears the tax man has caught up with me. We're going to have to make some sacrifices.
Eden (*with a laugh*) Well — as long as you don't sacrifice me.
Merlin Actually I was thinking of Kinnerton Street.
Eden The house? You mean sell it? But how will we entertain?
Merlin We'll twiddle our thumbs.
Eden And I'll be buried down here in the country?
Merlin With any luck.
Eden With any luck? What do you mean by that?
Merlin I might have to get rid of — well — this place, too.
Eden But where shall we live?
Merlin Well, I can live out of a suitcase.
Eden And what about me? Merlin, are you trying to tell me something? Are you thinking of leaving me?
Merlin My funny little darling, I married you until death us do part and I meant every word of it. I'm just saying you must pull your horns in. I mean, take that bloody horse ——

Eden Jimmy Thimble? Are you accusing me of extravagance? Who runs a Rolls and a Porsche?

Merlin For the image, my dear! You want the leading actor of the age running about in a Reliant Robin?

Eden Who has half a share in a yacht he never uses?

Merlin I get seasick.

Eden Who always flies Concorde? Merlin, your monthly cigar bill alone would keep my horse for a whole damn year.

Merlin The public expects it from me! You know quite well I'd rather stop at home with my stamp collection and trot around in bedroom slippers.

Eden Yes and who pays five thousand pounds for one tiny little postage stamp?

Charlie comes back but the others don't notice him

Merlin (*roaring*) Tiny? The size has nothing to do with it, you stupid little tart! My God, you have absolutely nothing between the ears. Astronomers would be enthralled by you. The first black hole on earth.

Eden Merlin, what's got into you? You're going right over the top.

Merlin Over the top! I've never been over the top in my life! How dare you say I'm going over the top — a cheap little actress. You're not fit to walk on the same planet as me — never mind the same stage!

Eden Merlin, please ——

Merlin I've never gone over the top in my life! That little bounder Kenneth Tynan once said I had, but what did he know? He was always over the top!

Eden Merlin, please, you know how much you need me.

Merlin Need you? Need you? I need you like stage fright. I need you like laryngitis. And if you're not careful I'll have you pine-boxed, do you hear? Pine-boxed!

Charlie (*after a tactful cough*) Excuse me.

Merlin Yes!

Charlie Excuse me — sorry — am I interrupting?

Merlin Charlie, dear boy. How long have you been standing there?

Charlie Me? Oh, I — oh — well ——

Eden It's OK, Charlie, come in. Merlin's just throwing one of his little tantrums. You'll get used to them. They don't mean a thing, do they, darling?

Merlin No. Sorry, my precious. Give me a kiss. There. My lovely poppet. (*He looks at his watch*) My word, is that really the time? I'd better go and dress if we're driving up to town. (*He starts up the stairs, then stops*) Oh, Eden, will you see that the spare room is in order? Charlie will be using it for the time being. And I'd be glad if you could keep him company for a few days.

Eden Keep him company?
Merlin Well, cook and clean for him, see he gets to bed on time. He's going to be a very busy lad.
Eden But Merlin ——
Merlin (*sharply*) Just see to it.

Merlin goes. Pause

Charlie Look, if my staying here's going to be awkward for you …
Eden No, Charlie, no trouble at all.
Charlie Does he often blow his top like that?
Eden It doesn't mean a thing, Charlie. Merlin wouldn't hurt a fly. Oh I know he can seem violent and unpredictable. I know he has this reputation for bar-room brawling — but scrape off the barnacles and a layer of marzipan is revealed.
Charlie Marzipan — what about his six wives?
Eden Yes, just like Henry the Eighth, isn't he? But I'm going to be his Catherine Parr. You know — the one who outlived him?
Charlie He's, um — he's always married money, hasn't he?
Eden Money? What a terrible thing to say. He's always married beautiful women — who just happened to be rich.
Charlie Are you rich?
Eden I was rich.
Charlie But now?
Eden It's all gone. Good heavens, why am I telling you all this? Merlin would be furious. You have a strange way of drawing a person out.
Charlie Sorry. I didn't mean to be nosey. Where's it all gone?
Eden My money? It's all gone into his productions — and just lately we've had a string of flops. Now no more questions.
Charlie No, sorry. How much did you have?
Eden One point eight million.
Charlie What!
Eden My daddy was very big in meat pies. Oh, I know what you're thinking. You're thinking that now my money's gone he'll start looking around. But you're wrong. Merlin would never leave me.
Charlie He'd be a fool if he did.
Eden Yes, he would. Because we've got a Californian marriage contract.
Charlie What?
Eden A watertight legal settlement drawn up by the toughest lawyer in Los Angeles. If Merlin ever tried to leave me, Charlie, it would cost him every penny he made for the rest of his life. The only escape clause is death. And who's going to live longest? Henry the Eighth or Catherine Parr? Hush, here he comes.

Merlin arrives downstairs dressed for London

Merlin OK, Charlie, my lad — are the ideas starting to bubble? (*Pause*)
What's wrong? Are you all right, Charlie? You look as white as a ghost.

Mozart's 40th plays as the Curtain *falls*

Scene 2

*It is three in the morning a week later and the cottage is in darkness. When
the lights come on the desk is a mess of papers and books piled about
Charlie's portable typewriter*

*The Mozart chimes are heard and after a while the light on the stairs comes
on and Eden descends in a nightdress and switches the downstairs lights on*

Eden (*tired and grumpy*) Yes, yes, all right, all right. (*She opens the front
door*)

Charlie comes in

My God, Charlie Nicholson, where on earth have *you* been? What time do
you call this?
Charlie (*a little the worse for drink*) Sorry, Eden, sorry, old girl. Hey, that
bell.
Eden What?
Charlie That doorbell.
Eden It's three o'clock in the morning. I've got to be up at the crack of dawn
to put a poultice on Jimmy Thimble.
Charlie Eden — that doorbell.
Eden You're drunk. Where have you been?
Charlie The Barracuda Club.
Eden Oh?
Charlie Funny old club that. I was the only customer. On the top of an old
deserted warehouse. It was just me and the croupier and lots of whisky on
the house. Funny old croupier, too. Spaniard with a handlebar moustache.
He took me for everything I'd got.
Eden Serves you right. How much?
Charlie Everything I'd got. Five thousand.
Eden Five thousand? Where did you get ——
Charlie The bell, the bell. Hold on a minute. That doorbell.
Eden What about the blooming doorbell?
Charlie A minute ago it gave me an idea. Now it's gone. What the hell was
it?

Eden I've no idea. I'm going to bed. Good-night.
Charlie No, wait. Would you mind going outside and ringing it?
Eden The doorbell? You're completely sozzled.
Charlie No, please, this is important. I'm starting to get an idea.
Eden What, for your play?
Charlie Could be, could be. Go out and ring that bell. Jog my memory.
Eden OK, but then I'm going to bed.

She goes out and rings the bell, then comes back in and closes the door

Well?
Charlie (*off in a world of his own*) Let me see — let me see. If the Police Commissioner telephoned Merlin — or if the Duchess of Lonsdale rang him — and while they were talking to him that doorbell started chiming — tiddle-pom tiddle-pom-tiddle-pom-pom — no, but hang about, how could Merlin be here and at Kinnerton Street at the same time? And where would you be?
Eden Wait a minute, What's all this? Are you writing a play about *us*?
Charlie About you? No, no. No, it's about — um — it's about a duchess who falls for a policeman. (*Suddenly slumping*) Oh, God, I'm not going to write anything. You know why? Because I've lost it. I can't do it any more. Eden, what's your favourite method of committing suicide?
Eden I don't know, but a hot bath comes into it somewhere.
Charlie Could you go and run me a hot bath?
Eden That bad, Charlie?
Charlie I'm a dead loss. I throw everything away. My wife — my money — even my tiny bit of talent. Oh, boy, is it the dark forces or is it just the malignant times?
Eden We all feel like that, Charlie, especially at three in the morning.
Charlie But I've lost it all, you see. I've lost exuberance. I've lost gusto. I've lost originality — zest — wit — ardour — panache — serenity — playfulness — magic — vivacity — courage — heart — optimism — hope. I've lost the point of it all.
Eden I'll go run the bath.

Pause

Charlie Eden, I love you. You're so bright, beautiful, playful, witty, zestful...
Eden I'll go make you some coffee.
Charlie No, don't go. Have you heard from Merlin today?
Eden Yes, he rang up tonight. Having a whale of a time.
Charlie Still in Venice?

Eden Yes, he flies home on Saturday. Oh, good heavens, I forgot to tell you. There was a phone call for *you.*

Charlie (*on guard*) When?

Eden About nine o'clock.

Charlie A call for me? There couldn't be. Nobody knows I'm here.

Eden Well Mr Forster does.

Charlie Mr Forster?

Eden Mr N. Forster.

Charlie N. Forster? (*Pause*) Oh God. Oh no.

Eden What's the matter?

Charlie I think you got the name wrong.

Eden No, N. Forster. I wrote it down.

Charlie Enforcer, Eden. Enforcer.

Eden N. Forcer?

Charlie As in one who enforces. An enforcer. What did he want?

Eden He said he'd drop in and see you some time. (*Pause*) What's the matter?

Charlie I think you'd better go and run that bath.

The doorbell chimes. Pause

Eden Good heavens, who's that?

The bell rings again

Well, I suppose I should go and see.

Charlie Yes. No. Hold on. I mean, three in the morning? It could be anybody.

Eden Yes, could be my grandma.

She goes and opens the door. A muffled exchange, then ——

Charlie, Mr N. Forster to see you.

Morten Rifles (*The Enforcer*) *enters*

Rifles Well, good-evening, good-evening, one and all. My name is Morten Rifles.

Charlie Oh — good-evening. Morning.

Rifles Excuse the lateness of the hour but am I addressing Mr Charlie Nicholson?

Charlie No.

Rifles Eh?

Charlie Yes.

Rifles Right. I represent Mr Horace Blinder and the shareholders of the Lucky Strike Casinos and Funeral Parlours Limited. An outstanding account of nine thousand, two hundred and fifteen pounds and thirty-two pence. Well now, Mr Nicholson, how would you like it?

Charlie I beg your pardon?

Rifles How would you like it? And where would you like it?

Charlie Sorry, I don't follow.

Rifles I do a complete service. Would you like it long or would you like it short? Would you like it here or would you like it in the open air? Some folks like it at a favourite spot — like a haunt of their youth or a place where they were happy once upon a time — such as their Oxford College or the place where they first got their end away. Would you like oak or pine or mahogany? Or maybe a nice inscribed pewter urn? It's all the same to me. Would you like horses and plumes and choirboys? Would you like Kensal Green or Golders Green? Would you like to be recycled as pigswill? Or would you prefer to be to be dismembered and distributed far and wide?

Charlie No — I — look here — isn't this a bit drastic?

Rifles Drastic? No, sir. It's just the usual. Not to worry. It won't hurt. Not much. I'm a craftsman. I could take your heart out so fast you wouldn't feel it. I've been in training ten weeks for this one. Swum one hundred and fifty miles, done two hundred miles on the bike, done three thousand sit-ups and one hundred and six rounds of sparring. All that pays off tonight, especially if you put up a contest. If you put up a contest this could be a terrific bout. Well what do you say?

Charlie Yes, right.

Rifles What, so it's a contest?

Charlie No, I'll pay up.

Rifles (*dismayed*) Pay up?

Charlie It's in this drawer. Excuse me, won't be a moment.

Charlie opens the desk drawer and brings out Merlin's revolver

Now then — will you please leave the premises?

Rifles Eh?

Charlie Now I'm warning you, this is loaded.

Rifles No it ain't.

Charlie What?

Rifles It ain't loaded.

Charlie What?

Rifles I can tell by the way you're carrying it. It's too light in the hand to be loaded.

Charlie We'll see about that.

Rifles OK, pull the trigger.

Charlie You want to be picking lead out of your navel?

Rifles You what? You've been watching too many late-night movies.

Charlie No, I haven't. I'm warning you, big boy. This is your last chance.

Rifles You can go take a flying jump.

Charlie Right, you've asked for it!

Eden Stop! Charlie, for God's sake, put it down! It's loaded!

Rifles Hold on. You mean it *is* loaded?

Eden Of course it's loaded — my husband keeps it there for burglars.

Charlie There — see — now go away or I'll shoot.

Rifles You'll shoot a debt collector going about his lawful business? That's a hard rap to beat. You want twenty years in the Scrubs?

Charlie What?

Rifles Twenty years.

Eden Put it down, Charlie. Please.

Charlie No.

Eden Charlie, *think!*

Charlie I have thought and I'd rather have twenty years in the Scrubs than end up as pigswill.

Eden All right, you win. You can have the money.

Charlie ⎫
         (*simultaneously*) What?
Rifles ⎭

Eden I said he can have the blooming money.

Rifles But I've swum one hundred and fifty miles, I've done three thousand sit-ups …

Eden I'll get it from my husband. He's in Venice at the moment but he'll fax it for you. First thing in the morning.

Rifles Just a minute. Can I use your blower?

Eden Of course. Please do.

Rifles (*goes to the phone and dials a number*) Hallo, could I speak to Uncle Horace? (*Pause*) Uncle Horace? This Charlie Nicholson's got a friend and she's making an offer. Yes. Payment in full. (*Pause*) Twelve noon at Rupert Street? OK. Bye-bye. (*He hangs up. Then to Eden*) The money has to be at seventy-two Rupert Street by noon tomorrow. That's in the West End.

Eden I know Rupert Street.

Rifles Twelve noon.

Eden I'll see it gets there.

Rifles If it don't, my dear, I'll come back to this room and strangle you with your own brassière.

Eden It'll be there.

Rifles This evening has been a terrible disappointment. Listen, Charlie Nicholson.

Charlie Yes?

Rifles Don't try to make a run because I'll be waiting outside this house until that money's handed over. So good-night, one and all.

He walks out of the front door

Pause

Charlie Right. That's it. I'm through. I'm finished.
Eden You what?
Charlie I quit, I'm getting out of here. I can't take any more. (*He starts collecting his stacks of paper, dictionary, thesaurus and portable typewriter*)
Eden But the play ——
Charlie How can I write a play with all this going on? The writer's mind is a delicate mechanism, precariously balanced. You need a little time, a little space, a little peace of mind. No wonder I can't write. Whenever I sit down to work there's a knock on my door. I come out to a quiet country cottage and I'm pursued by hoodlums. I get five thousand quid and it's immediately taken off me. I'm convinced now I wasn't meant to be a writer. God's designated my brain a no-go area for creative thoughts. Tell Merlin he'd be better off with Henry Savage's son-in-law. (*He marches to the door with his belongings piled in his arms*)
Eden Charlie, you can't leave.
Charlie Just watch me.
Eden That man will be waiting for you outside.
Charlie Oh. (*Coming back*) Tomorrow then — when the money's been handed over.
Eden But it won't be handed over, not if you refuse to do the play.
Charlie I've just told you, I can't do the play.
Eden You must do the play. Do it for me, Charlie. Please. I'll show my gratitude.
Charlie Show your gratitude?
Eden Merlin needs this play desperately. So do I. Otherwise we'll be destitute. I'll see you're not disturbed again. I'll pay off this enforcer. I'll straighten everything out with Merlin. Then you and I can see where we go from there.
Charlie You and I? What do you mean? Where could we go?
Eden What do you think I mean?
Charlie You don't mean — you and me? — You couldn't possibly mean —
Eden It's just that over these last few days, while we've been alone together — no, I'm not saying any more. I'm still Merlin's wife.
Charlie You're not thinking of leaving him?
Eden What would it matter to you if I did?
Charlie What would it matter to me? Eden, look, I'm no good at love

declarations — but I've been thinking — and it suddenly occurred to me — well — I often revile the century we live in, but it can't be such a bad century that has you in it.

Eden I think that's the nicest thing anybody's ever said to me and I'll treasure it as long as I live.

Charlie What's this about leaving him? Are you serious?

Eden Oh, I'm so mixed up. You see, when I first met him — no, I can't go into all that now.

Charlie No, go on.

Eden I was in an end of term play at RADA and just before curtain up the word went out, Merlin Foster's in front! He's looking for a young female lead for his latest blockbuster! Can you imagine that? Panic stations! Huge queues at the loo! Everybody gargling madly and mugging up their lines as though Shakespeare himself was out front. Don't know why *I* bothered, I only had a cough and a spit. Then later that night my doorbell rang and I got the shock of my life. Merlin was standing there with a big bunch of carnations and a cigar in his mouth. Anyway, he came in, just like a boy on his first date. I mean, the great Merlin Foster, courting me, because that's what he was doing. He said there was a small part for me in the play if I was willing to take it. I thought, that's strange, I only had a cough and a spit and I made a mess of the spit. Willing to take it! I'd have killed for it. Then two weeks into rehearsals he took me out to dinner, to break the news gently, as he put it. Break what news? I thought. Oh, God, he's going to fire me. But no, he said, it wasn't me. In fact I was wonderful, magnificent, unparalleled in theatrical history — although I only had a cough and a spit again. No, he said, one of the big backers had let him down and the show was off unless he could raise ninety thousand pounds within twenty-four hours. And before I knew what I was doing I'd opened my handbag and I was signing a cheque for ninety thousand. I think I knew in my heart of hearts what was going on, but I refused to admit it. I knew he was conning me but I thought, even if he is it's cheap at the price for a ticket to Mount Olympus. And anyway I'd get a good return on my investment because Merlin was highly bankable. The show was called *The Empty Years*, remember that one? No, you wouldn't. Should have been called the empty seats. It wasn't just unpopular. People were trampled to death in the rush to avoid it. That was the start of Merlin's long run of flops and I bankrolled all of them. And he never gave me another part. Not even a cough and a spit. And now I've an idea he's playing around with somebody else.

Charlie Somebody else?

Eden This trip to Venice. He usually takes me with him, but not this time. Why not? And then I suddenly remembered. There's a girl he used to know in Venice, an actress. I think she still lives there. He had a grand passion with her for years. I think he never got over it. (*Pause*) I'm not sure if I love him or just the idea of him, what he represents. They say fame's a terrific aphrodisiac, but *you're* not famous — and yet the moment I first set eyes on you — and just being near you, I get collywobbles and goosepimples. Well, what are you waiting for? Grab hold of me, kiss me.

Charlie (*taking her in his arms*) Oh, God, Eden, Eden.

Eden Oh, Charlie, this is impossible, what are we going to do?

A bang is heard upstairs

Did you hear that? What was that noise?

Charlie There's someone upstairs.

Eden What on earth — ? Quiet. They're coming down.

A disguised Merlin comes downstairs wearing a long black cloak and a grotesque Venetian carnival mask

Eden and Charlie cling together until Merlin removes the mask. He hands the mask to Charlie

Merlin A present from Venice, Charlie. A false face for a false friend.

Charlie False friend? Oh, no Merlin, you misunderstand ——

Eden Merlin, how on earth did you get in? How did you get up there?

Merlin I'm famous, my dear, for my dramatic entrances.

Eden How long have — um — you been back?

Merlin Just this minute. I thought I'd surprise you. We did the final scene in one take. Mr Bertolucci budgeted for two days shooting but I showed him how we could do it in one long tracking shot. Cinema histories will call it his most fantastic filmic moment. Yes, I caught the midnight plane. God knows what would have happened here if I'd waited for the one-thirty.

Eden What do you mean by that?

Merlin Shall I show you a mirror? It's written all over your foolish faces.

Eden You're wrong. Merlin! Something terrible happened to Charlie. He's had a dreadful shock. I was just comforting him.

Merlin That's enough! Go to bed!

Eden But Merlin — please — you don't understand.

Merlin To bed — you thumping strumpet!

Charlie Oh, now I say, Merlin ——

Merlin Silence! You're next on the menu.

Eden Merlin, honestly, I — oh, very well, believe the worst. You always do.

Eden runs off upstairs

Charlie Merlin, nothing happened, I swear to you, absolutely nothing.

Merlin, you must believe me. My life was threatened here, tonight. I was in a state of shock. Eden was just — just comforting me.

Merlin What? Your life threatened? Here? Why? Who?

Charlie By an enforcer.

Merlin An enforcer?

Charlie You know — a thug. My gambling debt. He came to collect.

Merlin A thug — has been here in my house? Who gave him this address?

Charlie God knows. That's what I've been wondering.

Merlin Savage!

Charlie What?

Merlin Good God alive. Henry Savage. Those bandits would stop at nothing to steal an idea.

Charlie But how could he have known I was ——

Merlin I tell you those sharks know everything. So you paid up, did you?

Charlie Paid up? No.

Merlin No?

Charlie I couldn't. This is all terribly embarrassing — the fact is — now promise you won't go off at the deep end. I'm broke.

Merlin Broke? What about the money I paid you?

Charlie I lost it. I just happened to drop into this — now keep cool, Merlin — well — I just happened to drop into this — um —

Merlin Savings bank?

Charlie Not exactly.

Merlin Building Society.

Charlie Casino.

Merlin Casino? The Barracuda Club? I see. You're as thick as Hadrian's wall, Charlie Nicholson. What are you?

Charlie As thick as Hadrian's wall.

Merlin Yes. Wait. You didn't give the thug his money. But you're still in one piece. What happened?

Charlie I don't know how you're going to take this next part. Eden said you'd pay.

Merlin I see. (*Pause*) Would it offend you if I asked if there was any sign of my play on the horizon?

Charlie The play? Ah, yes! Yes! I have an idea.

Merlin An idea?

Charlie Yes, a great idea. You're going to love it, Merlin.

Merlin I'd better. All right, tell me about this great idea.

Charlie (*improvising desperately*) Ah — well, Merlin it's all about — it's all about ——

Merlin Yes?

Charlie That doorbell.

Merlin That doorbell?

Charlie Yes, it's all to do with that doorbell — and your telephone — and the Police Commissioner — and the Duchess of Lonsdale. But don't ask me for details.

Merlin But what happens in the blessed thing?

Charlie I haven't quite worked that out yet.

Merlin Haven't worked it out?

Charlie No, don't worry, the facts sort of tumble into place, like an avalanche. They're starting to come at quite a lick now. Tell me — tell me something. How long does it take you to drive up to London from here?

Merlin About an hour, why?

Charlie The Police Commissioner. Do you know if he stops in at night?

Merlin Macnamara? No, he's always out, running after burglars. Except on Saturday nights, of course.

Charlie Saturday nights?

Merlin He's a football fan. Every Saturday night is sacred to *Match of the Night.*

Charlie *Match of the Night. Match of the Night!* That's perfect.

Merlin My God, what are you brewing up, Charlie?

Charlie Please — don't ask me anything else. But I guarantee — this has all the makings of an incredible plot.

Merlin One that would work in real life?

Charlie Definitely, definitely.

Merlin That's all I need to know. Very well, I'll give you one week to lick it into shape.

Charlie One week?

Merlin Never mind if the dialogue's a bit rough, we can tidy that up later. Meanwhile I'll pay off this man of yours. Agreed?

Charlie Thank you.

Merlin Now where do I pay this — enforcer?

Charlie Seventy-two Rupert Street — in the West End. By noon tomorrow.

Merlin Rupert Street? I walk down there every morning. I'm in town tomorrow and I'll drop it off before noon. Meanwhile you stay here and get cracking on that play. (*He takes out his chequebook*) Have you a pen?

Charlie hands Merlin a pen

Thank you. Now who do I make this out to?

Charlie Um — Horace Blinder.

Merlin (*chuckling as he signs*) Horace Blinder. (*Thoughtfully*) You know, I can understand that wife of mine consoling you after your shocking experience — but I fail to see why she had to undress to do so. What? Well I'm taking the little strumpet back to town tomorrow. She's given you enough consolation. (*Writing*) Horace — Blinder. Charlie, I've been meditating upon this murder of ours. I'd like you to make it as brutal and bloody and savage and sadistic as your imagination can conceive. Would you do that for me, please? Now — how much exactly did you say you wanted?

Mozart's 40th comes up as the CURTAIN *falls*

ACT II

Dusk. A week later

Charlie is asleep on the sofa, surrounded by dirty cups, saucers, plates and liquor glasses. There are sheets and balls of manuscript paper scattered everywhere and a big untidy script. He is woken by the ringing of the Mozart chimes

Charlie What? Oh. OK — I'm coming — OK. (*He opens the door*)

Merlin enters

Merlin Evening, Charlie.
Charlie Evening, Merlin. I thought you were in London.
Merlin Just popped down to see how you're getting on.
Charlie How are you?
Merlin Not so dusty, not so dusty.
Charlie How's Eden?
Merlin She's awfully well, thank you. Good God, you've made a hell of a mess of my cottage. The toils of creation, eh?
Charlie Sorry. When I'm working I get so wrapped up.
Merlin Not to worry if it's in the name of progress. Well, your week's up, my boy. Have you finished my lovely play?
Charlie Well, a first draft. (*Finding the big untidy script*) Here we are. Hot off the press. Excuse the lousy spelling.
Merlin Congratulations, my boy. Thank you. (*He puts on a pair of half-moon glasses and sits or lies on the sofa*) I see there's no title page.
Charlie No, I haven't typed it out yet. I'm going to call it *The Hit Man.*
Merlin *The Hit Man*? Oh no. It's called *The Final Twist.*
Charlie *The Final Twist*? You haven't even read it.
Merlin And if you don't shut up I never will. Perhaps you could have a go at tidying up while I glance though it. (*He turns a page*) Charlie, what's all this about my bloody doorbell?
Charlie Just read on. You'll see.

Charlie tidies up while Merlin reads. Then ——

Merlin, this title, how do you know there *is* a final twist before you've even read the damned thing?

Merlin If you haven't invented a final twist I'll put one in for you. It's a mere technicality.

Charlie Technicality? We're talking about my play.

Merlin My play, Charlie. I bought it, remember?

Charlie And I have no say in it?

Merlin I'm not unreasonable, Charlie. All I ask for is total control. A play like this depends on a final twist to keep the customers on their toes. Now tidy this pigsty and no more interruptions. (*He reads on for a while, then gives a yelp of rage*) Good God! What on earth do you mean by this?

Charlie What's that, Merlin?

Merlin Who is this mad old megalomaniac of an actor-manager?

Charlie I beg your pardon?

Merlin Who is this appalling conceited pompous swine?

Charlie It's you.

Merlin Me?

Charlie Yes.

Merlin Me? I never said such things as this.

Charlie Oh yes you did.

Merlin No I did not!

Charlie You told me to take notes. I took notes. It's you.

Merlin Good Lord, what a frightful rectum. I can't play a bounder like this. It would ruin my image. Just — tone him down a shade. Give him a touch of modesty. He *is* the greatest genius of the English-speaking stage. (*He turns over a page*)

Charlie Merlin, I've got to say something.

Merlin Well?

Charlie It's just that this plot — well — if somebody wanted to harm Eden — I mean really harm her — if this plot fell into the wrong hands — it could be about as dangerous as putting an open razor into a kiddies' play pen.

Merlin (*delighted*) I say, is that right?

Charlie And that's why I'd feel a whole lot happier if we could let Eden in on what we're up to.

Merlin Let her in on — ? Oh, God, you're not still harbouring those crazy notions about me? Oh, dear, I suppose I'd better own up.

Charlie Own up?

Merlin You see, Charlie, this play is in the nature of a Christmas present for the dear girl. A surprise package. I'm giving her the part, my boy. She plays the heroine.

Charlie Eden plays Eden?

Merlin Who else could play it so convincingly?

Charlie Right, right. You're right.

Merlin And telling her would spoil the surprise.

Charlie I see. Yes, you're right.

Merlin Look here, I can't plough through all this bumf with you chattering away. Just give me a quick run-down of the plot and I'll tell you what I think.

Charlie A run down of the plot? But won't that take away the element of surprise — when you read it? Oh — well — in a nutshell — it all revolves around the question of alibi.

Merlin Good. Carry on.

Charlie You see, Eden gets murdered up in London — at the house in Kinnerton Street — while you're down here at the cottage.

Merlin How do I do her in at Kinnerton Street while I'm down here at the cottage? Are we talking about a time bomb?

Charlie No, no.

Merlin What then?

Charlie You remember Norman Macnamara, the Police Commissioner?

Merlin Of course I do. I passed the time of day with him this morning as I took in the milk. What about him?

Charlie Well, Macnamara swears you were down here at the cottage when the murder was done. The Commissioner of the Met gives you your alibi.

Merlin Ah, the golden alibi. How's it done?

Charlie Well, before I begin, bear in mind the highly distinctive doorbell of this house.

Merlin The Mozart chimes?

Charlie Tiddy-pom tiddy-pom —

Merlin Yes, yes, I'll keep them in mind. Go on, Charlie.

Charlie Now if you're speaking on the telephone in this cottage and somebody happens to ring that doorbell, the Mozart chimes are overheard by the person on the other end of the line. And that tells him instantly, beyond all doubt, that you're speaking from this cottage. Am I right?

Merlin Well, if he happens to know this cottage and this doorbell, yes.

Charlie Does Macnamara know about the doorbell?

Merlin Let me see. Why, yes, I believe he does. We had him down for the weekend last summer — and yes — I believe he did remark on the bell. Tiddy-pom tiddy-pom — most people do.

Charlie Good. Now — we come to the murder itself. It takes place on a certain Saturday night at your house in Kinnerton Street. That morning you travel down here and leave Eden alone in the London house. When you depart from Kinnerton Street that morning — that fatal morning — you make sure that at least one neighbour sees you setting off and that he knows you're coming here. Ideally that person should be Macnamara.

Merlin Just to recap on the scoreboard. I depart from Kinnerton Street on

Saturday morning, leaving Eden behind me, and tell Norman Macnamara that I'm on my down way here. Right?

Charlie Right. Now when you get here you call at the village shop, or the post office or the pub — to establish that you've arrived. Buy a pound of sausages for your supper. Buy a bottle of wine.

Merlin Goose the postmistress.

Charlie That kind of thing. As long as your arrival here is noted by the locals. Meanwhile, back at Kinnerton Street, Eden is awaiting a visitor.

Merlin A visitor? What visitor?

Charlie When you left for the country that morning, you instructed her to stay behind because an important caller was expected at Kinnerton Street that night and only Eden could deal with her.

Merlin The visitor is a lady?

Charlie The visitor is an eccentric old woman who wants to invest some money in a new play.

Merlin An eccentric old angel?

Charlie Yes. The angel of death.

Merlin The angel of death. Go on, I like it. By George, I like it.

Charlie This old woman is due to call at ten o'clock that night. She's a terrible eccentric who won't have anything to do with men. She'll only deal with women.

Merlin Oh, you mean she's one of them?

Charlie No, no. But she has this longing to invest in a play and she knows a Merlin Foster epic is highly bankable. So she's arranged to turn up at the house that night carrying a plastic shopping bag stuffed with twenty-pound notes. You tell all this to Eden. Can you make her swallow it?

Merlin Leave it to me. She's the most trusting soul in creation.

Charlie Very well. On the stroke of ten Eden's doorbell rings. She opens the door. There stands the batty old angel — complete with plastic shopping bag. Eden lets her in and closes the door.

Merlin And now Eden is alone in the house — with the angel of death. Splendid. I'm getting goose bumps. Because of course it isn't an old woman she's invited into her parlour.

Charlie No, it isn't an old woman.

Merlin It's me!

Charlie You've got it.

Merlin It's Merlin Foster in drag!

Charlie And then without more ado you strangle her.

Merlin I like it, I love it.

Charlie And then you bring out a hacksaw, cut off her head and pop it in the shopping bag.

Merlin Oh now now. One moment, dear chap. A hacksaw? Oh, come, Charlie. Strangulation, yes, but fair's fair.

Charlie It's only a play, Merlin. (*Pause*) I said it's only a play.

Merlin Quite. But even so — what appalling barbarity.

Charlie You asked for barbarity. Make it bloody and brutal, that's what you said. Make it savage and sadistic.

Merlin So I did, so I did. Well, it's all most delicious so far. What next, my dear child?

Charlie Right. You walk out of Kinnerton Street with the head in the plastic bag. If anybody notices you leaving, so much the better. You go to your car, which is parked discreetly a few streets away, then head back here. But you only drive five miles and then you stop at a public call box and telephone Macnamara. You tell him you're calling from this cottage. You say you're somewhat anxious about Eden. You tell him she rang up about half an hour before and said there was a batty old woman in the house who wouldn't go away. You advised her to ring him — Macnamara — right away to come along and get rid of her. Eden said she'd do that pronto. However, you'd been trying to ring Eden again to see if all was well but you could get no reply. So would he kindly pop round to see if all was well? And at that moment your doorbell starts chiming. Tiddle-um tiddle-um tiddle-pom-pom — and of course Macnamara at the other end hears the Mozart chimes.

Merlin Ah, but surely, I'm not at home. I'm in some dreary wayside telephone kiosk. So how could my doorbell …?

Charlie Just let me finish. Your doorbell starts chiming — tiddle-um tiddle-um tiddle-pom-pom — and you say to Macnamara, "Hold on, old boy. There goes my doorbell. I'll just pop along and see who's there. With luck it could be Eden herself." And then you go away for a minute, leaving him dangling. Then you come back to him and you're out of control, you're hysterical, you tell him something horrible's happened. You've just found Eden's head on the doorstep.

Merlin Good Lord, that'll put the wind up him, won't it? Because it's certainly put the wind up me. But hold on a moment.

Charlie Yes?

Merlin I see a big hole in this story.

Charlie Oh yes?

Merlin Something of a magician I might be — but how can I be here in this cottage and in a distant telephone box at the same time?

Charlie But you're *not* here. You *are* in a distant telephone box.

Merlin So how does Macnamara hear my confounded doorbell?

Charlie You play it to him.

Merlin I play it to him?

Charlie Just a moment. (*He brings a little black cassette player from the drawer*) You play it to him — on this.

Merlin What's that?

Charlie A cassette player. Listen — I taped this last night. (*He switches on* *the cassette player and we hear a recording of the Mozart chimes*) All you have to do is play it to Macnamara while you're in that phone box.

Merlin Great heavens.

Charlie You're barely five miles from Kinnerton Street but he's absolutely convinced you're down here — fifty miles away.

Merlin My God, so he is.

Charlie So Macnamara rushes next door and breaks the door down and finds Eden's headless corpse. Now imagine the scene at Kinnerton Street. All hell breaks loose. There's only one thing Macnamara can be sure of — that you didn't do this murder. Wasn't he talking to you on your own phone only minutes ago?

Merlin So he was, so he was.

Charlie Meanwhile you've driven back here like crazy and by the time the police turn up to take charge of the head you've changed out of your make-up, you've burned the cassette and the old woman's clothes, you're the baffled, grieving husband, a figure to be pitied and consoled. And best of all you're completely in the clear. And that is the plot. Well?

Pause

Merlin How horrible, fantastic, incredible. How wonderful. But listen, old chap ——

Charlie Yes?

Merlin Wouldn't this make more effective theatre if the old woman were to call at Macnamara's house first — before the murder?

Charlie Before the murder?

Merlin Yes, what if she were to call at Macnamara's house and ask for Eden? And Macnamara explains that she's come to the wrong house — that Eden lives next door. And then the old woman apologizes and goes on her merry way. Her merry murderous way. You follow? It clinches the story that Eden has a late caller and that it was an old bag lady. My God, I want to play this part. I want to see Macnamara's face when I come calling at his door dressed as a sweet little old lady.

Charlie Hold on, hold on. Aren't you getting a little carried away?

Merlin Carried away?

Charlie We're talking about a play.

Merlin I know that. But first we rehearse.

Charlie We rehearse? How do you mean?

Merlin I go through every motion.

Charlie Every motion?

Merlin Next Saturday night. No good hanging about. I happen to know that the Duke of York's is falling vacant in December, just in time for the Christmas trade.

Charlie You go through every motion next Saturday night?

Merlin I put it on the test bench. I time it with a stopwatch. I find out for certain if this little plot of yours actually works in real life.

Charlie No, Merlin ——

Merlin Quiet. Let me think. Yes, I travel down here next Saturday morning. I spend the day doing what? Yes, I could deadhead the roses, spray some sweet peas. And the folks down in the village will spot me — a distant noble figure toiling from noon to twilight. Then darkness falls and I slip quietly away, the angel of death, taking care to drive out of here quietly and unseen through the back lanes.

Charlie And what's Eden doing all this time?

Merlin Eden is sitting at home at Kinnerton Street, waiting for a crazy old angel.

Charlie You're really going to tell her an angel is on the way?

Merlin Exactly as it says in your script. This is a full technical rehearsal.

Charlie And you really call on Macnamara — dressed in drag?

Merlin I must. It's in the script. And the kindly policeman directs me to Eden's door.

Charlie And then what do you do, when Eden opens it?

Merlin I step inside.

Charlie And then what? (*Pause*) You don't strangle her? You don't — cut off ——

Merlin Be serious, Charlie. I thought I'd cured you of such nonsense.

Charlie So what do you tell her — once you get inside?

Merlin I tell her who I am, if she hasn't twigged already. I tell her I'm pulling a little stunt and everything will shortly be explained. And then I kiss her good-night, leave the premises and swing into phase two — the drive home, the telephone call to Macnamara.

Charlie You really do stop on the way home? You actually telephone Macnamara and play the tape down his earhole?

Merlin It's in the script.

Charlie Merlin, there's something wrong here. I don't like it.

Merlin Well, you bloody well wrote it!

The Mozart doorbell chimes

Merlin Oh, blast, who the hell's that? (*He opens the* door)

Eden comes in

Ah, darling, how lovely to see you.

Eden (*tearfully*) Merlin.

Merlin I thought you were attending an audition.

Eden (*trying to suppress tears*) No, something else came up. Something in the post. I thought you'd like to see it right away. (*She hands him a letter*)

Merlin But this is addressed to me — and you've opened it.

Eden (*tearfully*) It was posted in Venice and it's in a woman's handwriting. Of course I opened it. You've taken up with Magliano again. You spent the night with her when you went to work with Bertolucci. How could you, Merlin?

Merlin Oh, that! Is that all? My dearest, darling girl, it was all shatteringly innocent. I know it looks bad, but I simply used Miss Magliano's villa instead of a hotel.

Eden You promised me that was all over years ago.

Merlin But it is. Miss Magliano and I are just friends, mere friends.

Eden Not according to that letter. It's so juicy she must have been trampling grapes when she wrote it.

Merlin But you must make allowances for Latin overstatement. They make a laundry list sound like a passionate declaration.

Eden That's not a laundry list, it's an aria by Puccini!

Merlin Exactly what I'm saying. Who in his right mind could take such a woman seriously?

Eden I could. She's arriving in London on Monday. No doubt her enormous bust will be arriving the day before.

Merlin Well, it's quite simple, my dear. She's going to invest a lovely lump of money in Charlie's play.

Eden (*a further blow*) Oh. And I suppose that means she's going to play the lead.

Merlin Possibly. And now if you'll excuse me I need something from the toolshed. Charlie, give Eden a drink. She's a little upset.

Merlin leaves

Charlie Drink?

Eden No thank you.

Charlie Magliano? *Lucia* Magliano? The film star?

Eden He discovered her when she was a little sixteen-year-old waitress in Naples. Of course, that was about a hundred years ago. He gave her a tiny part in one of his films. She never got rich enough to qualify as one of his wives, but now — now ——

Charlie Yes?

Eden She married that enormous Italian shoe manufacturer — well he wasn't enormous but his shoes were — oh you know what I mean …He was killed in a car crash last year — left her millions and millions. And now she's coming to London. And Merlin's got her slated as wife number seven, I know he has. Well, he won't get rid of me as easily as all the others.

No. I've got a Californian marriage contract. And the only escape clause is death. So I'm all right, aren't I, Charlie?

Pause. Charlie is gobsmacked

Charlie, I asked you a question.

Merlin returns, carrying a hacksaw wrapped and hidden in sacking

Merlin Eden, my darling, I've been thinking about Magliano.

Eden I know you have — for the last twenty years!

Merlin It's true. For years and years I carried a vision of the divine Lucia in my head. But going to her villa cured me of all that. She's nothing but an old Roman ruin. You're so young. You helped to bring me back to life. And when I see you standing there — so fresh and innocent — so eager and lovely — I know I'm the luckiest man in all creation. Now come on, we're going back to town and I'm going to buy you the biggest diamond in London.

Eden I don't want a diamond! I just want you!

Merlin Then your wish is granted. Hand on heart, I'm yours for life.

Eden What have you got there, Merlin?

Merlin This? Oh it's my hacksaw.

Eden Hacksaw? What do you want with a hacksaw?

Merlin To tell you the truth, darling, I've a got a job of work to do at Kinnerton Street. (*Pause*) And next Saturday night, Charlie …

Charlie Yes?

Merlin *Match of the Night*, Charlie. *Match of the Night*!

Mozart's 40th comes up as the CURTAIN *falls*

SCENE 2

The following Saturday. Late evening

Before the CURTAIN *rises we hear the signature tune for the football. (Not the* Match of the Day *tune, which is prohibited due to copyright difficulties) At* CURTAIN *up the football programme is just starting on television. Charlie is on the telephone. He switches off the television*

Charlie (*in desperate mood*) Yes, hallo, could you try a number for me? … 0171-229-0879. … Yes I've been dialling it for over two hours but I keep getting no reply. … Well, there should be someone in! I know she's in! …Yes, thank you, it's desperately urgent, please hurry!

*He goes to the drinks cabinet and pours a drink with shaking hands when the
doorbell rings and he spills it . He goes and opens the door — not knowing
what to expect — and gives a startled cry as ——*

*Merlin sails in wearing a frock and carrying a Sainsbury's plastic carrier
bag*

Merlin (*in an old woman's voice*) Hallo, hallo, Charlie my dear boy.
Charlie Merlin, where have you been? (*Pause as he notices Merlin's bag*)
What's in that bag?
Merlin The scarlet deed is done.
Charlie What?
Merlin (*urgently*) Get pencil and paper. Make a note of the time.
Charlie Time? Time, right. (*He snatches up pen and paper*) Merlin, what's
in that bag?
Merlin Write down the time. Don't hang about! Write down everything!
Charlie I am, I am! Where's Eden? How is she? Is she all right?
Merlin Eden is — I'll come to that. I'll come to that.
Charlie But is she all right? Just tell me she's all right. My God, look!
Merlin What's the matter?
Charlie Blood. There's blood on your dress.
Merlin What?
Charlie Blood on your dress.
Merlin Oh yes, I got in a fight.
Charlie Fight? Who with?
Merlin Is the bathwater hot?
Charlie Yes. What's in the bag, Merlin? There's something big and heavy
in that bag.
Merlin Observant of you.
Charlie And blood on that dress.
Merlin I told you. I had a fight.
Charlie At Kinnerton Street?
Merlin No, on the bloody Guildford by-pass.
Charlie Guildford by-pass?
Merlin I got stuck in a tailback on the way home and you know how it is.
Charlie Yes?
Merlin Everything came to a grinding halt. Well, the usual chorus of
mindless hooting went on and I turned round at one point and gave the v-
sign to some imbecile behind me who kept hooting at *me*. Next thing I knew
he was climbing out of his car and coming to my door. Well, when he saw
I was a little old lady in a print frock he contented himself with kicking my
door in, but I wasn't having any of that. I jumped out and walloped him on
the chin. Laid him out cold.

Charlie Merlin, what's in the bag?

Merlin Charlie, you are a genius. It worked.

Charlie Worked? What do you mean exactly?

Merlin I carried out your plan. To the letter. But my God, it wasn't easy.

Charlie What wasn't easy?

Merlin None of it. It was hard. Bloody hard. You write a hard part for an actor, Charlie. And for an actress. Oho, yes, sir, and for an actress.

Charlie Merlin will you stop — stop prevaricating — and tell me what's in that bag?

Merlin A trophy of war. My father was a cannibal king up the Amazon, you know. A head hunter. It must be in the genes.

Charlie Never mind the genes, what's in the bag?

Merlin takes a cigar from a case on the desk and lights up, taking his time

Merlin Take notes. This is important. Now here's a strange thing. I almost lost my nerve. Convincing an audience in the theatre is one thing, but in real life it's a different story. I had definite butterflies as I approached Macnamara's door. Not only that, but I'd forgotten the carriage lamps.

Charlie Carriage lamps?

Merlin On either side of Macnamara's door. When he opened up they bathed me in light. God, I nearly bolted. But no, I told myself, you must go through with this. Play it for real, sink into the part, forget Merlin Foster and actually become that old woman. Because the one you've got to convince most of all is not the audience but yourself. So when Macnamara's eyes bored into me, when his sharp copper's gaze roved over my painted face in the full glare of those blazing lights — I gazed straight back and put my face to the light and smiled, smiled a little roguishly, and made my inquiry — fully convincing myself that I was the old woman — and thus convincing him! And so he pointed the way to Eden's house and withdrew with a polite (*in a yokel's voice*) "Good-night." But the wonder of it all was that Eden was convinced, too.

Charlie Eden? Until you told her, you mean?

Merlin Told her?

Charlie Explained.

Merlin Explained? Why should I do that?

Charlie You mean — she didn't recognize you — and you didn't enlighten her?

Merlin Enlighten her? Oh no. Quite out of the question. Because by then, you see, I was lost in my role. Quite, quite lost. Mysterious how a part can take you over. I was no longer Merlin Foster. I was the angel of death. The role had been written. I had been cast for the part. It had to be played, to the bitter end.

Charlie What's in the bag, Merlin?
Merlin Here you are. Why don't you take a look? Smelling salts are on the desk. (*He hands Charlie the bag*)
Charlie What's this? It's heavy.
Merlin Thirty-four ounces, I believe.
Charlie Thirty-four ounces?
Merlin So I believe. But I must get moving. You did say the water was hot, didn't you? If all goes according to plan, the police should be here in five minutes. Let them in, will you?
Charlie The police?
Merlin When they arrive you will corroborate my story. I was here all day and all night. You can swear to that.
Charlie Merlin, you've got to be joking.
Merlin You were here when my doorbell rang. You were here when I opened the door and stumbled over the head on the step.
Charlie Merlin ——
Merlin You heard a car speeding away. You succoured and solaced me in my distress. And if you wish to tell a different tale, my boy, remember that you are my accomplice. Not only that, but you dreamed up the whole wicked scheme yourself. Accessory before the fact I believe they call it. Yes, well, I must go and change. (*He starts upstairs*) Oh, pop the head on the doorstep, will you, and burn the bag.

He goes off upstairs

Charlie (*to himself, examining the bag but afraid to open it*) My God, what's he done? No, he can't have. But what about the blood? Oh, my God.

The Mozart bell chimes out

Oh, no. The police. Oh no.

After some dithering, wondering what to do with the bag and finally hanging on to it, he opens the door

Eden steps inside

Eden Hi, how's the big gambler?
Charlie Eden! Oh, Eden! For God's sake! Am I glad to see you!
Eden Just back from Sainsbury's, I see.
Charlie Sainsbury's?
Eden The bag.
Charlie Bag? Oh, this, no, Sainsbury's will be closed by now.

Eden What have you got in there?

Charlie This bag? Oh, I was just putting it away.

Eden How's the play going?

Charlie Play? What play? Oh, play! You know, for a moment I'd forgotten I was writing a play.

Eden Well, is it finished?

Charlie Finished? To tell you the truth I'm still a bit mystified about the ending.

Eden Well why don't you take a look in the bag?

Charlie Bag?

Eden The bag might help you.

Charlie I beg your pardon?

Eden Charlie, dear, take a quick glance in the bag. The answer might be in there.

Charlie This bag?

Eden Yes.

Charlie Eden? What do *you* know about this?

Pause

Merlin (*coming down*) Charlie, that damned water's icy cold! Expect me to wash off bloodstains in a freezing — oh, Eden, my dear.

They kiss

Eden Hi, Merlin. How did it all go?

Merlin Oh first class. Like clockwork. Not a hitch. One might say it's in the bag.

Eden In the bag, yes, so I see.

They all look at the bag in Charlie's hand for a long moment

Congratulations, darling.

Merlin Now don't go congratulating me. Charlie's the boy.

Eden Yes, congratulations, Charlie. Jolly well done

Pause, while it all sinks in on Charlie

Charlie Eden! So you knew! You knew all the time. And you let me go on thinking …

Eden Yes? Let you go on thinking what, Charlie?

Charlie Thinking that you — thinking that he ——

Eden Thinking that it might all be for real?

Charlie (*blustering*) For real? Now come off it. Good heavens, if you think
I'm that sort of person ——

Eden But you had your suspicions, Charlie. Come on, own up. And you
never thought of warning me.

Charlie I did try to warn you! I've been trying to get you on the bloody
blower all night.

Eden So you did have your suspicions.

Charlie No! Look here, I know what you're up to, you've both been trying
to manipulate me in some — some sordid exercise, but I never fell for it,
not for a second, no!

Eden You were ready to let my head be cut off, Charlie.

Charlie No I was not!

Eden And I'd grown so fond of you. I thought you were fond of me.

Charlie OK! That's enough of the joke.

Merlin Joke? He still hasn't twigged. This is no joke, Charlie. Don't you see
what we've done? We've proved that a murder plan can be constructed by
a writer and carried out by an actor in every particular. I followed every
step. I did every deed as you dictated.

Charlie All but one.

Merlin Why? What have I left undone?

Charlie The plan was to murder your wife.

Merlin Yes?

Charlie Only she's still alive. She's standing there.

Merlin Oh, you mean Eden.

Charlie Yes, who else?

Merlin But Eden is not my wife.

Pause. Charlie looks from one to another

Charlie You're not his …

Eden No, Charlie. I'm not his wife.

Charlie Not his wife? So who — who is your wife?

Merlin My wife is Dorothea Southgate, the distinguished Catholic novelist.

Charlie You're not divorced?

Merlin Dorothea didn't believe in divorce.

Charlie So — so where is she now?

Merlin At Kinnerton Street. Well, her body's at Kinnerton Street. But her
head ——

Charlie (*laughing uncertainly*) Now come on. I mean — the game's over.
We've all had a good laugh. We've established I'm an idiot. Please don't
labour the joke.

Eden Open the bag, Charlie.

Charlie Now that's enough! This is all getting very childish! End of joke!
Stop messing about!

Merlin He's afraid of what he'll find.

Eden He's frit.

Charlie (*with false bravado*) Very well, I'll open it. You can't scare me. (*He
opens the bag and stares inside for a long moment*) Oh God. Oh my God.

Merlin Meet my wife.

Charlie Oh no.

Merlin I hope you're making a mental note of all this, Charlie. Just imagine
the impact on an audience.

Charlie The only audience you'll have will be a judge and jury at the Old
Bailey.

Merlin Oh no, it won't come to that. Now I believe I owe you one final
payment.

He goes to the desk drawer, brings out the revolver and points it at Charlie

Chekhov, you know, always maintained that if you showed a gun in act one
you were obliged to fire it in act three.

Eden Merlin, what are you up to?

Merlin Quiet, my dear.

Eden But Merlin — no!

Merlin There comes a time in the life of a play, my dear Charlie, when the
author has to retire to the darkness and put his little creation into the hands
of the actors and that moment has now arrived.

Eden Merlin, what the hell's this? What the hell *is* this?

Merlin Be quiet, Eden, or I'll have to deal with you, too. Good heavens, this
fellow cares nothing for you. He was going to let you die.

Eden No, he was just weak! He was just confused!

Merlin We can't afford weakness and confusion. And now I'd like you to
walk out to the well, Charlie.

Eden The well? What are you up to? No, you can't! This is a joke, isn't it?

Merlin It's no joke, my darling. He knows too much. Outside, Charlie.

Charlie No. Wait, wait, just think. If I disappear I'll be traced to this house.

Merlin There's nothing to connect you with this house. No-one knew you
were coming here. Cast your mind back and you'll remember I made that
a condition of our first meeting.

Charlie (*suddenly remembering*) Ah!

Merlin Well?

Charlie N. Forster!

Merlin What?

Charlie The enforcer — the thug — the man sent by my bookie.

Merlin I'm afraid he won't help.

Charlie I wouldn't be so sure.

Merlin But I am. (*In the voice of The Enforcer*) Would you like horses and plumes and choirboys? Would you like Kensal Green or Golders Green? Would you like to be recycled as pigswill? Or would you prefer to be to be dismembered and distributed far and wide?

Merlin and Eden enjoy a good chuckle

Charlie Oh no.

Merlin Oh yes.

Charlie That was you.

Merlin It was a busy night for me. I also played the croupier.

Charlie Eh?

Merlin At the Barracuda Club. "Steek or tweest, senõr. Steek or tweest?" It was embarrassingly simple to relieve you of your money.

Charlie (*admiringly*) You absolute bastard.

Merlin Now please do as I ask and walk out to the well.

Eden Merlin, there's no call for this! He won't give us away! Will you, Charlie?

Merlin Won't give us away? Look at him. Even if he was on our side he'd never have the bottle to see it through. We've got to bluff our way past the police and possibly through the law courts. It's going to call for acting abilities of the highest calibre. Sorry, Charlie, but every man to his trade. Outside, please.

Charlie suddenly jumps him. There is a struggle and shouting and then two gun-shots. Merlin collapses to the floor

Merlin (*a dying man*) Oh dear. Oh dearie me.

Eden (*kneeling beside him*) Merlin, oh, Merlin.

Merlin He took me by surprise.

Eden Charlie, what have you done? Merlin, Merlin …

Merlin This wasn't in the script, you know.

Eden Merlin! — Oh — I think he's gone.

Charlie Oh, no. Are you sure?

Eden There's no pulse. Yes, he's gone. Oh, the fool, the damned idiotic fool. I warned him about that gun. I told him to use blanks, but no, he was such a ridiculous perfectionist. He had to rehearse everything, down to the last detail.

Charlie Rehearse? What are you talking about, rehearse? He was going to kill me.

Eden No, don't you see, that was just another twist! The final twist! It was just another part of the play! He wasn't going to harm you. He just wanted to see your reactions when you were faced with a gun. He wanted to get it right, don't you understand?

Charlie That was a play? Only a play? He wasn't going to kill me?

Eden No, no!

Charlie Good Lord, the futility of it all. Just for a play. But wait—what about his wife?

Eden I'm his wife.

Charlie But — what about that? There's a woman's head in that bag — covered in blood.

Eden A fake.

Charlie A fake?

Eden Just a very clever theatrical fake.

Merlin (*feebly*) Eden — Eden —

Eden Merlin! Oh, my darling.

Merlin Life — life in the old dog — yet.

Eden Hush, my darling, hush.

Merlin Charlie? You there, Charlie?

Charlie Yes, Merlin?

Merlin Make a note.

Charlie A note?

Merlin Famous last words.

Charlie Merlin, you've got to rest.

Merlin Now write this down, write it down,

Charlie (*he finds pencil and paper*) OK, Merlin.

Merlin Dying words of Merlin Foster.

Charlie Yes?

Merlin We make our entrance — we make a balls-up — we make our exit.

He dies with a spectacular death rattle

Eden He's gone.
Charlie Yes, he's gone.

Long pause

Merlin (*leaping to his feet*) And there I think we roughly have it. And there the curtain slowly falls.

Charlie Merlin! My God, Merlin!

Merlin I think it's all going to work splendidly, don't you? Make us all a fortune.

Charlie Good God! You old rogue! I thought you were dead! Never do that to me again.

Eden Merlin, how did I do? Was I OK in that last scene? I mean, have I got the part?

Merlin My darling, you were born for the part.

Charlie You incredible old fraud! I say, just one last question.

Merlin Go ahead, my boy.

Charlie That *was* the final twist? Please.

Merlin Final twist? Oh, yes, you've finally exhausted my powers of invention. Oh — (*picking up the bag*) — there is just the matter of this splendid head.

Charlie Oh? What about it?

Merlin Well it's a pity we can't use it in the actual production.

Charlie Oh? Why can't we?

Merlin It *is* my wife. And they go off in the hot weather, you know. Better pop it down the well. Here you are — catch.

He chucks the head to Charlie

Mozart's 40th blazes up as ——

the Curtain *falls*

FURNITURE AND PROPERTY LIST

Further dressing may be added at the director's discretion

ACT I

On stage: Desk with drawer. *In it*: revolver, small black cassette player
On it: box of cigars, pen, pencil, paper, diary, chequebook, telephone
Television
Drinks cabinet with drinks and glasses
On shelf: books, two Oscars
Sofa

Off stage: Riding hat, riding crop (**Eden**)
Portable typewriter (**Charlie**)
Personal belongings (**Charlie**)
Stacks of paper, dictionary, thesaurus (**Stage Management**)

Personal: Cigar lighter (**Merlin**)
Wrist-watch (**Merlin**)
Pen (**Charlie**)

ACT II

On stage: Dirty cups, saucers, plates and liquor glasses around sofa
Sheets and balls of manuscript paper
Big untidy script

Off stage: Letter (**Eden**)
Hacksaw wrapped in sacking (**Merlin**)
Sainsbury's plastic carrier bag. *In it*: fake head (**Merlin**)

Personal: Half-moon glasses (**Merlin**)

LIGHTING PLOT

Property fittings required: nil
Interior. The same throughout

ACT I, SCENE 1. Mid-morning

To open: Bring up general mid-morning effect

No cues

ACT I, SCENE 2. Night

To open: Darkness, when ready bring up light on stairs

Cue 1   **Eden** switches on light   (Page 14)
             Bring up lights on downstairs

ACT II, SCENE 1. Dusk

To open: Dusk effect

No cues

ACT II, SCENE 2. Late evening

To open: General evening effect. As CURTAIN rises bring up flicker
             effect on television

Cue 2   **Charlie** switches off the television   (Page 33)
             Cut flicker effect

EFFECTS PLOT

ACT I

Cue 1   *Before* Curtain *rises sparkling performance of* Mozart's   (Page 1)
        40th Symphony. *When ready cross-fade to electric doorbell*
        chiming first twenty notes of Mozart's 40th

Cue 2   **Merlin**: "… white as a ghost."   (Page 14)
        Mozart's 40th *plays, when ready open* Scene 2 *with*
        cross-fade to Mozart chiming doorbell

Cue 3   **Eden** exits   (Page 15)
        Mozart chiming doorbell

Cue 4   **Charlie**: "… run that bath."   (Page 16)
        Mozart chiming doorbell

Cue 5   **Eden**: " … who's that?"   (Page 16)
        Mozart chiming doorbell

Cue 6   **Eden**: "… what are we going to do?"   (Page 21)
        Sound of bang upstairs

Cue 7   **Merlin**: "… say you wanted?"   (Page 24)
        Mozart's 40th *comes up*

ACT II

Cue 8   *When ready, Mozart chiming doorbell*   (Page 25)

Cue 9   As **Charlie** switches on cassette player   (Page 29)
        Sound of cassette player recording of Mozart
        chiming doorbell

Cue 10   **Merlin**: "… you bloody well wrote it!"   (Page 31)
        Mozart chiming doorbell

Cue 11   **Merlin**: "*Match of the Night.*"   (Page 33)
        Bring up Mozart's 40th. *When ready cross-fade to the*
        football signature tune. As Curtain *rises, fadefootball*
        music to background television volume for start of
        programme. When Charlie turns the television off cut
        television effect